NATIVE AMERICAN
WISDOM

NATIVE AMERICAN
WISDOM

Edited by

KRISTEN MARÉE CLEARY

FALL RIVER PRESS

Copyright © 1995, DoveTail Books

This 1996 edition published by Fall River Press,
by arrangement with DoveTail Books.

Design copyright © Ziga Design, LLC

Fall River Press
122 Fifth Avenue
New York, NY 10011

ISBN-13: 978-0-7607-0320-5

Printed and bound in China

11   13   15   17   19   18   16   14   12   10

Front cover photograph: Placating the spirit of a slain eagle; back cover:
Kutenai duck hunter; *page 8*: Berry-gatherers; *page 25*: Chief Joseph; *page
50*: Coming for the bride (photographs by Edward S. Curtis, courtesy
of the Prints and Photographs Division, Library of Congress).
Page 38: Mother and daughter at Jemez Pueblo (photograph by Jesse L.
Nusbaum, negative # 61712, courtesy of the Museum of New Mexico).

CONTENTS

FOREWORD

When the first Europeans landed in the "New World," the inhabitants called them *Awaunageesuck:* the strangers. Native American society comprised hundreds of nations speaking several hundred languages. They were united by such common bonds as their respect for nature and kinship, intense spirituality, courage and hardihood, and highly developed skills as hunters, farmers, gatherers, fishermen and artisans. These skills and beliefs were maintained through centuries of adversity, and passed on to new generations despite dwindling numbers and resources.

During the twentieth century, the native nations have seen a resurgence, through a reversal of the population decline, restored freedom to practice sacred traditions, and a newly reclaimed pride in this rich heritage. The *Awaunageesuck* have, at last, begun to appreciate and learn the values of these great nations. A glimpse of the ancient and profound wisdom informing the lives of America's first people can be found in the following pages.

KRISTEN MARÉE CLEARY

1996

ONE

AT ONE
WITH NATURE

At One with Nature

A deep reverence for Mother Earth lies at the heart of the beliefs and traditions of the native nations of North America. Whether for inhabitants of lush, fertile lands, arid desert, ocean shores, or the harsh subarctic, nature is the peoples' bountiful provider, and earth the sustainer of life. As seen in the lifeways of ancient hunter-gatherers, trappers, and fishers, through centuries of adaptation to new circumstances, homelands, and techniques, a profound respect for earth's fellow-creatures — both philosophical and practical — permeates Native American society.

According to many of the origination stories that have been passed down in tribal legend, the earth not only sustains life, but is sacred because it was the original source of all life. An Iroquois creation story tells that:

"In the beginning, people lived beyond the sky, because deep waters covered the entire earth. Then, a pregnant woman fell from the Sky World toward the water. Ducks and geese broke her fall with their wings and carried her to the Great Turtle, master of all animals, and set her on his back. The Turtle ordered the other animals to bring earth from the bottom of the water and cover his back that she might have land to live upon."

Will you ever begin to understand the meaning of the very soil beneath your feet? From a grain of sand to a great mountain, all is sacred. Yesterday and tomorrow exist eternally upon this continent. We natives are guardians of this sacred place.

Peter Blue Cloud, Mohawk

Deer, I am sorry to hurt you, but the people are hungry.

Choctaw Hunter's Prayer

What is man without the beasts? If all the beasts were gone, men would die from great loneliness of spirit, for whatever happens to the beasts also happens to man. All things are connected. Whatever befalls the earth befalls the children of the earth.

Seathl, Duwamish chief

At One With Nature

from

THE GREAT LAW OF THE HODENOSAUNEE CONFEDERACY

Whenever the statesmen of the League shall assemble they shall offer thanks to the earth where men dwell, to the streams of water, the pools and lakes, to the maize and the fruits. The eagle…is able to see afar. If he sees in the distance any danger threatening, he will at once warn the people of the league.

Iroquois

And when I quit the city and came home, I found myself where I was supposed to be before. Everything is beautiful, the mountain changes, every, every time I look at it, it changes. The water, don't change the sound—the air is the same, flows. The spirit, when the tree is shaking then I realize that the spirit is there…People live not knowing, all they know is the top of their shoes today. They don't know the glory, the what we're living underneath. Beauty, nighttime, daytime that is what the things are that I value.

Jimmy Reyna, Taos Pueblo

from THE BLANKET AROUND HER

The white wind
that encircles her is a part
just as
the blue sky
hanging in turquoise from her neck...

Joy Harjo, Creek

PRAYER TO A CEDAR TREE

Look at me, friend!
I come to ask for your dress
Since there is nothing you cannot be used for.
I come to beg you for this,
Long-life maker.

Kwakiutl

I love the land and the buffalo, and will not
part with it. I love to roam over the prairies. There
I feel free and happy.

White Bear, Santana

Our land, our religion, and our life are one. It is upon this land that we have hunted deer, elk, antelope, buffalo, rabbit, turkey. It is from this land that we obtained the timbers and stone for our homes and kivas.

Hopi creed

My people, before the white man came you were happy. You had many buffalo to eat and tall grass for your ponies—you could come and go like the wind. When it grew cold you could journey to the valleys of the south, where healing springs are; and when it grew warm, you could return to the mountains of the north. The white man...dug up the bones of our mother, the earth. He tore her bosom with steel. He built big trails and put iron horses on them.

Wovoka, Paiute

I buried my father in that beautiful valley of the winding waters. I love that land more than all the rest of the world.

Chief Joseph, Nez Percé

When I was young and strong our country was full of game which the Great Spirit sent us to live upon. The lands that belonged to us were extended far beyond where we hunted…When your fathers asked us for land, we gave it to them, for we had more than enough.

Gayashuta, Seneca

I have been to the end of the earth.
I have been to the end of the waters.
I have been to the end of the sky.
I have been to the end of the mountains.
I have found none that are not my friends.

Navajo proverb

AT ONE WITH NATURE

from CALLING MYSELF HOME

This land is the house
we have always lived in.
The women,
their bones are holding up the earth.

Linda Hogan, Chickasaw

The old people came literally to love the soil. They
sat on the ground with the feeling of being close to
a mothering power. It was good for the skin to
touch the earth, and the old people liked to
remove their moccasins and walk with their bare
feet on the sacred earth. The soil was soothing,
strengthening, cleansing, and healing.

Luther Standing Bear, Lakota Sioux

We are the stars which sing,
We sing with our light;
We are the birds of fire,
We fly over the sky.
We look down on the mountains
This is the song of the stars.

Algonquian poem

The whole Southwest was a House Made of Dawn.
It was made of pollen and rain.
The land was old and everlasting.
There were many colors on the hills and on the
    plain,
And there was a dark wilderness on the mountains
    beyond.

Southwestern song

When we show our respect for other living things,
they respond with respect for us.

Arapaho proverb

For the Lakota there was no wilderness. Nature was not dangerous but hospitable, not forbidding but friendly.

Luther Standing Bear, Lakota Sioux

A long time ago this land belonged to our fathers; but when I go up to the river I see camps of soldiers on its banks. These soldiers cut down my timber; they kill my buffalo; and when I see that, my heart feels like bursting.

Satanta, Kiowa

When a man eats salmon by the river, he sings the salmon song. It is in the river in the roasting in the spearing in the sharing in the shoring in the shaking shining salmon. It is in the song too.

Kwakiutl poem

Our land is more valuable than your money. It will last forever. It will not even perish by the flames of fire. As long as the sun shines and the waters flow, this land will be here to give life to men and animals. We cannot sell the lives of men and animals. It was put here for us by the Great Spirit and we cannot sell it because it does not belong to us.

Crowfoot, Blackfoot

Before eating, always take a little time to thank the food.

Arapaho proverb

The roots of the tree of [the white man's] life have not yet grasped the rock and soil.... But in the Indian the spirit of the land is still vested; it will be until other men are able to divine and meet its rhythm. Men must be born and reborn to belong. Their bodies must be formed of the dust of their forefathers' bones.

Luther Standing Bear, Lakota Sioux

At One With Nature

We must go beyond the arrogance of human rights. We must go beyond the ignorance of civil rights. We must step into the reality of natural rights because all the natural world has a right to existence. We are only a small part of it. There can be no trade-off.

John Trudell, Santee Sioux
(from his address at the Survival Gathering, 1980)

All plants are our brothers and sisters. They talk to us and if we listen, we can hear them.

Arapaho proverb

These lakes, these woods, and mountains were left us by our ancestors. They are our inheritance; and we will part with them to none. He, the Great Spirit and Master of Life, has provided food for us in these spacious lakes, and on these woody mountains.

Pontiac, Ottawa chief

If we hold our lands, there will always be a turkey, or deer, or a fish in the streams, for those young who will come after us.

Doublehead, Creek

For more than seventy years I have hunted in this grove and fished in this stream, and for many years I have worshipped on this ground. Through these groves and over these prairies in pursuit of game our fathers roamed, and by them this land was left unto us as a heritage forever.

Senachwine, Potawatomi

Great Spirit! You lived first, and you are older than all need, older than all prayer. All things belong to you—the two-legged, the four-legged, the wings of the air and all green things that live.... I am sending you a voice, Great Spirit, my Grandfather, forgetting nothing you have made, the stars of the universe and the grasses of the earth.

Black Elk, Oglala Sioux

The Crow country is a good country. The Great Spirit put it exactly in the right place. It has snowy mountains and sunny plains, all kinds of climate and good things for every season. When the summer heats scorch the prairies, you can draw up under the mountains, where the air is sweet and cool, the grasses fresh, and the bright streams come tumbling out of the snowbanks. There you can hunt the buffalo, or trap beaver in the streams. And when winter comes on, you can take shelter in the woody bottoms along the rivers; there you will find buffalo meat for yourselves, and cottonwood bark for your horses. The Crow country is in exactly the right place. Everything good is to be found there. There is no place like Crow country.

Arapooish, Crow chief

God created this Indian country and it was like He spread out a big blanket. He put the Indians on it. They were created here in this country, and that was the time this river started to run. Then God created fish in this river and put deer in these mountains and made laws through which has come the increase of fish and game. Then the creator gave us Indians life; we awakened and as soon as we saw the game and fish we knew that they were made for us. For the women God made roots and berries to gather, and the Indians grew and multiplied as a people. When we were created we were given our ground to live on, and from that time these were our rights.... My strength is from the fish; my blood is from the fish, from the roots and the berries. The fish and the game are the essence of my life. Whenever the seasons open I raise my heart in thanks to the Creator for his bounty that this food has come.

Meninock, Yakima chief

Our dead never forget the beautiful world that gave them being.

Seathl, Duwamish chief

TWO

COURAGE AND STRENGTH

COURAGE AND STRENGTH

During the five hundred years since the arrival of the first European colonists, Native Americans have seen the beloved, hallowed earth of Turtle Island— a name used by some tribes for America—invaded, appropriated, deforested, and polluted. Dispossessed of their homelands, removed far from the territories that sustained their lifeways, many of the first peoples were devastated by disease and warfare. Those who survived were forced to accept new ways, to learn another's language, schooled in a religion unknown to them, and forbidden to practice traditional sacred rites.

That the values and beliefs held by many of the five hundred nations have endured and reemerged is testament to the unshakable tenacity of the keepers of the faith. Stories of the courage, defiance, and wisdom of tribal elders, holy people, warriors, and wise women have been passed down through the ages, providing inspiration to successive generations. Black Hawk, a great Sauk leader, encouraged a fighting spirit in his community in 1832 with these words:

"The Great Spirit is the friend and protector of the Sauks, and has accompanied me as your war chief upon the warpath against our enemies, and has given me skill to direct you and you the courage to achieve a hundred victories over our enemies."

Where [are] the Narraganset, the Mohican, the Pakanoket and many other once powerful tribes of our people? They have vanished before the avarice and oppression of the white man, as snow before a summer sun.

Tecumseh, Shawnee chief

I am a red man. If the Great Spirit had desired me to be a white man he would have made me so in the first place. Now we are poor but we are free. No white man controls our footsteps. If we must die, we die defending our rights.

Sitting Bull, Hunkpapa Sioux

Today is a good day to fight— today is a good day to die.

Crazy Horse, Oglala Sioux

COURAGE AND STRENGTH

I am in your power. Do with me what you please.
I have done the white people all the harm I could;
I have fought them, and fought them bravely: if I
had an army, I would yet fight…but I have none;
my people are all gone. I can now do no more than
weep over the misfortunes of my nation.

Red Eagle, Creek
At his 1814 surrender to Andrew Jackson

Your forefathers crossed the great water and
landed on this island. Their numbers were small.
We took pity on them, and they sat down among
us. We gave them corn and meat. They gave us
poison in return.

Sagoyewatha (Red Jacket), Seneca

Since you are here as strangers, you should rather
confine yourselves to the customs of our country
than impose yours upon us.

Wicomesse leader, 1633

That was our hunting ground and you have taken it from us. This is what sits heavy [on our] hearts and the hearts of all nations.

Cornstalk, Shawnee chief

There was a time when our people covered the whole land as the waves of the wind-ruffled sea cover its shell-paved floor. But that time has long since passed away with the greatness of tribes now forgotten. I will not mourn over our untimely decay, nor reproach my paleface brothers with hastening it.

Every part of this soil is sacred in the estimation of my people. Every hillside, every valley, every plain and grove, has been hallowed by some sad or happy event in days long vanished.

Seathl, Duwamish chief, 1855

Sell a country! Why not sell the air, the clouds and the great sea, as well as the earth? Did not the great spirit make them all for the use of his children?

Tecumseh, Shawnee chief

COURAGE AND STRENGTH

Here no one fears to die in war…keep this in mind, O princes.

Aztec Scribe

The might of our arms will be known and the courage of our brave hearts.

Aztec scribe

For up here where we live, our life is one continuous fight for food and for clothing and a struggle against bad hunting and snowstorms and sickness. That is all I can tell you about the world, both the one I know and the one I do not know.

Inuit woman, 1920s
(To ethnologist Knud Rasmussen)

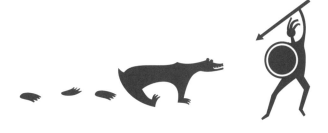

If they are to fight, they are too few;
if they are to die, they are too many.

Chief Hendrick, Mohawk
(French and Indian War, 1755)

Our lives are in the hands of the Creator. We are
determined to defend our lands, and if it be his
will, we wish to leave our bones upon them.

Tecumseh, Shawnee chief

You might as well expect the rivers to run back-
ward as that any man who was born free should be
contented to be penned up and denied liberty to
go where he pleases.

Chief Joseph, Nez Percé

Why is it that Apaches wait to die—that they carry their lives on their finger nails? They roam over the hills and plains and want the heavens to fall on them. The Apaches were once a great nation; they are now but few, and because of this they want to die and so carry their lives on their finger nails.

Cochise, Chiricahua Apache chief

We are minded to live at Peace: If we intend at anytime to make War upon you, we will let you know of it, and the Reasons why we make War with you; and if you make us satisfaction for the Injury done us, for which the War is intended, then we will not make War on you. And if you intend at any time to make War on us, we would have you let us know of it, and the Reasons for which you make War on us, and then if we do not make satisfaction for the Injury done unto you, then you may make War on us, otherwise you ought not to do it.

Anon., Lenape

We want no white men here. The Black Hills belong to me. If the whites try to take them, I will fight.

Sitting Bull, Hunkpapa Sioux chief

A nation is not conquered until the hearts of its women are on the ground.

Traditional Cheyenne saying

I am sending a voice, Great Spirit, my Grandfather, forgetting nothing you have made, the stars of the universe and the grasses of the earth. You have said to me, when I was still young and could hope, that in difficulty I should send a voice four times, once for each quarter of the earth, and you would hear me. Today I send a voice for a people in despair.... Hear me, not for myself, but for my people; I am old. Hear me that they may once more go back into the sacred hoop and find the good red road, the shielding tree!

Black Elk, Lakota Sioux

COURAGE AND STRENGTH

I am king in my land, and it is unnecessary for me to become the subject of a person who has no more vassals than I. I regard those men as vile and contemptible who subject themselves to the yoke of someone else when they can live as free men. Accordingly, I and all my people have vowed to die a hundred deaths to maintain the freedom of our land. This is our answer, both for the present and forevermore

> *Timucuan, Acuera chief*
> *(to Hernando de Soto, 1539)*

I like it well. I shall die before my heart is soft or I have said anything unworthy of myself.

> *Canonchet, Narragansett*
> *(before an English firing squad, 1676)*

If this is the way they pray, that is bullets through people's hearts, I hope they will not pray for me; I should rather be excused.

> *William Apess, Pequot*

I have been among the French at Quebec and at Three Rivers; they taught me the foundation of their doctrine. But the more thoroughly I examined their mysteries, the less clearly I saw the light. They are tales invented to inspire us with true beliefs of an imaginary fire and under the false hope of a good which never will come to us, to engage us in inevitable unhappiness.

Agouachimagan, Algonquian

If you English were our friends as you pretend you are, you would not suffer us to starve as we did.

Madokawando, Penobscot

It is no longer good enough to cry peace, we must act peace, live peace, and live in peace.

Shenandoah proverb

Courage and Strength

When I look upward, I see the sky serene and happy; and when I look on the earth, I see all my children wandering in the utmost misery and distress.

> *Mashipinashiwish, Ojibwa*
> *(On an epidemic of smallpox, 1760s)*

We heartily recommend Union and a good agreement between you.…Our wise forefathers established Union and Amity between the Five Nations. This has made us formidable.…We are a powerful Confederacy; and by your observing the same methods our wise forefathers have taken, you will acquire such strength and power.

> *Canassatego, Onondaga*
> *(1775, on the proposed founding of the United States)*

When you first came to our coasts, you sometimes had no food; we gave you our beans and corn, and relieved you with our oysters and fish; and now, for recompense, you murder our people.

> *Anon., Montauk*

Brother, when you were young, we were strong; we fought by your side; but our arms are now broken. You have grown large; my people have become small. Brother, my voice is weak; you can scarcely hear me; it is not the shout of a warrior, but the wail of an infant. I have lost it in mourning over the misfortunes of my people. These are their graves, and in those aged pines the ghosts of the departed.

Colonel Webb, Choctaw

Your forefathers crossed the great waters, and landed on this island. Their numbers were small. They found friends and not enemies. They told us they had fled from their own country for fear of wicked men, and come here to enjoy their religion. They asked for a small seat. We took pity on them, granted their request, and they sat down amongst us. We gave them corn and meat. They gave us poison in return. The white people had now found our country.

Sagoyewatha (Red Jacket), Seneca

THREE

TIES OF
KINSHIP AND
NATIONHOOD

Motherhood—the bearing, nurturing, and raising of the next generation—is a deeply respected role that is considered critically important in Native American society. But, according to an Omaha proverb, it takes an entire village to raise a child. While children are encouraged and taught by the wider community as well as by their parents to learn and grow, elderly people, too, are accorded the respect and protection of all around them.

Beyond the affection and warmth of living relationships, family and clan ancestors are also remembered and honored—and sometimes consulted for spiritual help or advice by means of traditional ceremonial rites. Despite the diversity of culture and belief among the native nations, the bonds of family and clan are universally strong.

A profound sense of kinship and belonging can be seen in times of peace and plenty as much as in times of adversity. On the one hand, family is a source of personal identity, a loving community, a place of joy, and a cause for celebration. On the other, a fierce sense of protection toward kin and nation is second nature when trouble threatens. In the words of a Sioux proverb:

With all things and in all things, we are relatives.

from LONG DIVISION: A TRIBAL HISTORY

We are bought and divided
into clay pots; we die
on granite scaffolding
on the shape of the Sierras
and lie down with lips open
thrusting songs on the world.

Wendy Rose, Hopi/Miwok

There are stories and stories.... There are the songs,
also, that are taught. Some are whimsical. Some are
very intense. Some are documentary.... Everything
I have known is through teachings, by word of
mouth, either by song or by legends.

Terrance Honvantewa, Hopi

You think the Axe-Makers are the eldest in the
country and the greatest in possession. We Human
Beings are the first, and we are the eldest and the
greatest. These parts and countries were inhabited
and trod upon by the Human Beings before there
were any Axe-Makers.

Sadekanaktie, Onondaga

TIES OF KINSHIP AND NATIONHOOD

I come to a powwow to be an Indian, to get a sense of myself. This is part of Indian spirituality, to help each other and to celebrate with each other. When I come to powwows, I gain strength to carry on with my life.

Rachel Snow, Assiniboin

My son, you are now flesh of our flesh and bone of our bone. By the ceremony performed this day, every drop of white blood was washed from your veins; you were taken into the Shawnee nation…you were adopted into a great family.

Black Fish, Shawnee
(to Daniel Boone, 1778)

THE FOUNDING OF TENOCHTITLÁN

Behold, a new sun is risen,
A new god is born,
New laws are written,
And new men are made.

Aztec poem
(on the founding of the Aztec capital, now Mexico City)

Under the shade of this Tree of Great Peace we spread the soft white feather down of the globe this-tle as seats for you, Atotarho and your cousin lords. There shall you sit and watch the council fire of the Confederacy of the Five Nations. Roots have spread out from the Tree of Great Peace. These are the Great White Roots, and their nature is Peace and Strength. If any man or nation shall obey the laws of the Great Peace, they shall trace back the roots to their source, and they shall be welcome to take shelter beneath the Tree of the Long Leaves. Into the depth of the earth, down into the deep undercurrents of water flowing into unknown regions, we cast all weapons of war. We bury them from sight forever and plant again the Tree.

> *Deganawida, Iroquois*
> *(From the opening of the Constitution of the*
> *Confederacy of the Five Nations)*

I am a Shawnee. My forefathers were warriors. Their son is a warrior. From them I take only my existence. From my tribe I take nothing. I have made myself what I am.

> *Tecumseh, Shawnee chief*

The Apache seem to be very strong when somebody
dies. When somebody dies, when you hear thunder
way over there—so that you just hardly hear it—
that means that the white cloud is taking him to
another world. They travel for many days, and then
sometimes on the fourth day it rains. When that
rain drops on you, they are touching you.

Philip Cassadore, Apache

from REMEMBER

Remember your birth, how your mother struggled
to give you form and breath. You are evidence of
her life, and her mother's, and hers.
Remember your father, his hands cradling
your mother's flesh, and maybe her heart, too
and maybe not.
He is your life also.

Joy Harjo, Creek

We must let you know we love our Children too well to send them so great a way, and the Indians are not inclined to give their Children learning. We allow it to be good, and we thank you for your Invitation; but our Customs differing from yours you will be so good as to excuse us."

Canassatego, Iroquois orator

Brothers: The Seneca nation see that the Great Spirit intends that they shall not continue to live by hunting, and they look around on every side, and inquire who it is that shall teach them what is best for them to do.

Cornplanter, Seneca

When you gave us peace, we called you father, because you promised to secure us in possession of our lands. Do this, and so long as the lands shall remain, the beloved name will remain in the heart of every Seneca.

Cornplanter, Seneca
(from an address to George Washington, 1790)

Ties of Kinship and Nationhood

I first address you from a dead chief, who, when he was about to die, called us to him and charged us never to part with our lands.... I love the land on which I was born, the trees which cover it, and the grass growing on it. It feeds us well. I am young, and by hunting on my land, can kill what I need, and sustain my women and children in plenty.

Como, Potawatomi chief
(from an address to George Washington, 1793)

At the center of the old Sioux society was the tiyospaye, the extended family group, the basic hunting band, which included grandparents, uncles, aunts, in-laws, and cousins. The tiyospaye was like a warm womb cradling all within it.

Mary Crow Dog, Lakota Sioux

Remember that your children are not your own, but are lent to you by the Creator.

Mohawk proverb

The Spaniards charged the crowd with their iron lances and hacked us with their iron swords. They slashed the backs of some. They hacked at the shoulders of others, splitting their bodies open… The blood of young warriors ran like water; it gathered in pools. And the Spaniards began to hunt them out of the administrative area buildings, even starting to take those buildings to pieces as they searched. Great was the stench of the dead. Your grandfathers died and with them died the son of the king and his brothers and kinsmen. So it was that we became orphans, O my sons! So we became when we were young. All of us were thus. We were born to die!

> *Aztec scribe*
> *(on the Spanish attack at Tenochtitlán, 1520)*

To us the ashes of our ancestors are sacred and their resting place is hallowed ground. Our religion is the traditions of our ancestors—the dreams of our old men, given them in the solemn hours of night by the Great Spirit; and the visions of our sachems; and is written in the hearts of our people.

> *Seathl, Duwamish chief*

Ties of Kinship and Nationhood

I want to do something even if it's gonna be in a small way for all the people, for my Muskokee people. When I think about that, I think about Opothleyahola. I think about him, what he did say always comforts me. He says, "Even though I'm gone, always remember, mention my name, and one of these days, there'll come a time that Muskokee people will live like they used to." That's what I think about, that's what my heart lies upon.

Sam Procter, Creek

Grandfather, I pray to you.
Grandfather, don't let me be
taken away.
My people need me,
as I need them.

Leonard Crow Dog, Lakota Sioux

For it is in peace only that our women and children can enjoy happiness and increase in numbers. We should, therefore, extend the hand of friendship from tribe to tribe, until peace shall be established between every nation of red men within the reach of our voice. Brothers, when we call to mind the only associations which endeared us to the land which gave birth to our ancestors; and when we see that our ancient fire there has been extinguished, and our people compelled to remove to a new and distant country, we cannot but feel sorry; but the designs of Providence, in the course of events, are mysterious—we should not, therefore, despair of once more enjoying the blessings of peace in our own homes. Brothers, let us so then act that the peace and friendship which so happily existed between our forefathers, may be forever preserved; and that we may always live as brothers of the same family.

John Ross, Cherokee chief

A man or woman with many children has many homes.

Lakota Sioux proverb

FOUR

DESTINY:
DREAMS AND
VISIONS

Destiny: Dreams and Visions

The unity and simplicity of their lifeways fostered in the earliest native peoples a deep acceptance of both seen and unseen forces. When a Native American youth went into the forest or the desert to seek a supernatural talisman (the vision quest), he or she received instruction from a foreordained guardian spirit, or *manitou*. These spirits were sometimes ancestors, sometimes intermediaries between the individual and the Great Spirit; they had the power to transform themselves into various visible forms. Fasting and sleeplessness were rewarded by a dream or vision of the guardian spirit, who stayed with the person throughout his or her life, protecting him from evil forces and guiding decisions for the common good.

Dreams and prophecies lie at the heart of native spirituality, as the spirit is believed to travel to other realms, returning with guidance that fulfills the "secret desires of the soul." Strength, understanding, and peace are found through inner experience, whether waking or sleeping. Beyond the individual, the spiritual world is universal and infuses the whole of the natural world: it informs earth and skies, breathes life into mountains and waters, and imparts a soul to every living creature born of the earth — each to return to the earth. In the words of an Arapaho proverb,

If we wonder often, the gift of knowledge will come.

What we are told as children is that people when they walk on the land leave their breath wherever they go. So wherever we walk, that particular spot on the earth never forgets us, and when we go back to these places, we know that the people who have lived there are in some way still there, and that we can actually partake of their breath and of their spirit.

Rina Swentzell, Santa Clara Pueblo

I had a dream that the earth was dark. And every time I would point my finger, a light would come on. The lights were many different sizes, and shapes, and colors. I asked the creator spirit what these lights were. The spirit told me these were people who would come and study with me as apprentices.

Sun Bear, Chippewa, 1980

Everything the Power does, it does in a circle.

Lakota proverb

SPIRIT SONG

There is fear
In the longing for loneliness
When gathered with friends,
And longing to be alone.
Iyaiya-yaya!
There is joy
In feeling the summer
Come to the great world,
And watching the sun
Follow its ancient way.
Iyaiya-yaya!
There is fear
In feeling the winter
Come to the great world,
And watching the moon
Now half-moon, now full,
Follow its ancient way.
Iyaiya-yaya!
Where is all this tending?
I wish I were far to the eastward.
And yet I shall never again
Meet with my kinsmen.
Iyaiya-yaya!

Inuit

I have seen the time when my dreams were true; when I had seen moose or beaver in sleep, I would take some. Now our dreams and our prophecies are no longer true—prayer has spoiled everything for us.

Algonquian hunter

The Black Hills have great significance to the Lakota and Dakota people. It is said that the prayer of the white man, the Lord's Prayer, has meaning because the Black Hills is on earth as it is in heaven. It mirrors the constellations.

Patricia Locke, Hunkpapa Sioux/Chippewa

The boy cried and cried. The blood came out, and finally he died. With his tears our lakes became. With his blood the red clay became. With his body our mountains became, and that was how Earth became.

Taos Pueblo creation story

Destiny: Dreams and Visions

The people came through four worlds and then up from the bottom of the Lake of Changing Waters. They were led by First Man and First Woman and their children, the Changing Twins. One twin formed a food bowl from the clay of the stream bed, while the other fashioned a water basket from reeds. Stones shaped themselves into tools and weapons, and mahogany branches became digging sticks. Finally, they fashioned hoes from the shoulder blades of deer. They found the agricultural Kisani people and traded their materials for seeds. They learned to build dams, and soon water spread to where it was needed.

Navajo creation story

from GRANDMOTHER

From beyond time,
beyond oak trees and bright clear water flow,
she was given the work of weaving the strands
of her body, her pain, her vision
into creation, and the gift of having created,
to disappear.

Paula Gunn Allen, Laguna/Sioux/Lebanese

The ancient world was inhabited by animals who spoke and acted like humans. A vicious monster who lived by one of the waterways kept the animals in fear by eating any who came near. Finally, the Coyote killed the monster by jumping down his throat and cutting up his heart with a flint. He then cut the monster into pieces, forming a different tribe from each part.

Nez Percé legend

GHOST DANCE SONG

The whole world is coming,
A nation is coming, a nation is coming,
The Eagle has brought the message to the tribe.
The father says so, the father says so.
Over the whole earth they are coming.
The buffalo are coming, the buffalo are coming,
The Crow has brought the message to the tribe,
The father says so, the father says so.

Sioux

DESTINY: DREAMS AND VISIONS

A VISION OF STRANGERS

Men of strange appearance have come across the great water. They have landed on our island [North America]. Their skins are white like snow, and on their faces long hair grows. These people have come across the great water in wonderfully large canoes which have great white wings like those of a giant bird. The men have long and sharp knives, and they have long black tubes which they point at birds and animals. The tubes make a smoke that rises into the air just like the smoke from our pipes. From them come fire and such terrific noise that I was frightened even in my dreams.

Ojibwa prophet

Chinigchinich then proceeded to make a new people from clay, and they became the Indians of today. He placed these Indians in groups all over the country and gave them what they needed to survive. He gave them their languages and their customs and all was good.

Gabrielino creation story

A long time ago my father told me what his father had told him, that there was once a Lakota holy man, called Drinks Water, who dreamed what was to be. He dreamed that a strange race would weave a web all around the Lakotas. He said, "You shall live in square gray houses, in a barren land." Sometimes dreams are wiser than waking.

Black Elk, Oglala Sioux

Sometimes you look at a thing and see only that it is opaque, that it cannot be looked into. And this opacity is its essence, the very truth. So it was for me with this mask. The man inside was merely motion and he had no face, and his name was the name of the mask itself.

N. Scott Momaday, Kiowa

The Great Spirit has made us what we are: it is not his will that we should be changed. If it was his will, he would let us know; if it is not his will, it would be wrong for us to attempt it, nor could we, by any art, change our nature.

Seneca proverb

Imagine a Seneca storyteller. He is a hard-working man with signs of advancing age on his face. It is eveningtime. He waits for us, and we come up to him and say, "Grampa, tell us ghost stories." He would blow out a big puff of smoke, and he would begin: "Now this happened one time…"

Duwayne Leslie Bowen, Seneca

SONG OF LAMENTATION

I am like the quetzal bird, I am created in the
house of the one only God; I sing sweet songs
among the flowers; I chant songs and rejoice in
my heart.
The fuming dewdrops from the flowers in the field
intoxicate my soul.
I grieve to myself that ever this dwelling on earth
should end.

Ancient Nahuatl Poem

Treachery darkens the chain of friendship, but truth makes it brighter than ever.

Conestoga proverb

Life is as the flash of the firefly in the night, the breath of the buffalo in winter time.

Blackfoot proverb

I came over the trail of many moons from the setting sun.... I come with one eye partly open, for more light for my people who sit in darkness. I go back with both eyes closed. How can I go back blind to my people?

Anon., Nez Percé, 1831

Beauty before me
Behind me
Below me
Above me
All around me
In beauty, I have spoken.

Annie Kahn, Navajo

When I was in the other world with the Old Man, I saw all the people who have died. But they were not sad.... It was a pleasant land, level, without rocks or mountains, green all the time, and rich with an abundance of game and fish. Everyone was forever young.

After showing me all of heaven, God told me to go back to earth and tell his people you must be good and love one another, have no quarreling, and live in peace....

> *Wovoka, Paiute*
> *(His vision of the Ghost Dance revival, 1889)*

We stand somewhere between the mountain and the ant.

> *Onondaga proverb*

We will dance when our laws command us to dance, we will feast when our hearts desire to feast…. It is a strict law that bids us dance. It is a strict law that bids us distribute our property among our friends and neighbors. It is a good law. And now, if you are come to forbid us to dance, begone.

> *Anon., Kwakiutl, 1886*
> *(Protesting the anti-potlatch law)*

We must dance the balance of this moon, at the end of which time the earth will shiver very hard. Whenever this thing occurs, I will start the wind to blow. We are the ones who will then see our fathers, mothers, and everybody. We, the tribe of Indians, are the ones who are living a sacred life.

> *Short Bull, Sioux*

Life is not separate from death. It only looks that way.

> *Blackfoot proverb*

DESTINY: DREAMS AND VISIONS

We do face the sun and pray to God through the sun, asking for strength to complete the Sun Dance, and that our prayers will be heard. We are able to see the sun with our eyes completely open. It doesn't blind us, and in it we see visions.

Frank Fools Crow, Lakota Sioux

It seems to us that from the earliest times, man's natural state was to be free as our grandfathers told us and we believe that freedom is inherent to life. We recognize this principle as the key to peace, respect for one another and the understanding of the natural law that prevails over all the universe and adherence to this law is the only salvation of our future on the planet, Mother Earth.

Oren Lyons, Onondaga, 1987

When you lose the rhythm of the drumbeat of God, you are lost from the peace and rhythm of life.

Cheyenne proverb

The grandfathers
and the grandmothers
are in the children;
teach them well.

Ojibwa proverb

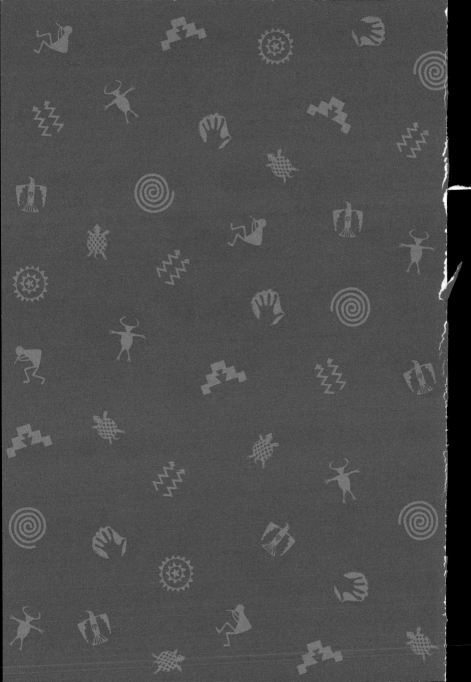